Disclaimer

This book is based on real-life experiences, personal reflections, and stories shared by migrants. However, some names, places, and identifying details have been changed to protect the privacy and safety of those involved.

Any resemblance to actual people, living or dead, not explicitly referenced, is purely coincidental.

The views and opinions expressed in this book are solely those of the author and do not necessarily reflect the positions of any public or private institution with which she has been affiliated.

The purpose of this book is to offer a human lens on the complexities of migration and to foster empathy for those who cross borders with courage, fear and dignity.

A HUMANITARIAN LENS ON IMMIGRATION

PAPER DOORS

SELENE PARTIDA

First edition, 2025

Paper Doors: A Humanitarian Lens on Inmigration

ISBN: 979-9-9996459-1-3

Printed and made in Mexico
Impreso y hecho en México

To my father, Eduardo Partida
and my mother, Maggie Estrada,
for leaving behind their land, their story,
and their roots: to plant hope in foreign soil
and give me —even in uncertainty—more than they had.

For showing me that migration
is an act of love.

This book is theirs too.
Selene Partida

Table of Contents

Author's Note 13

Introduction 17

Chapter 1.
The Crossing 19

Chapter 2.
Two Worlds 27

Chapter 3.
Between Shadow and Hope............................... 37

Chapter 4.
Forced Migration.. 45

Chapter 5.
Modern Slavery.. 51

Chapter 6.
Return Migration 57

Chapter 7.
Binational Families... 63

Chapter 8.
Citizen Children, Undocumented Parents 67

Chapter 9.
Daily Uncertainty... 73

Chapter 10.
30 and 40 Years Without Documents:
The Human Cost of Migratory Limbo 77

Chapter 11.
When Death Comes Far Away 85

Chapter 12.
The Silent Grief We Carry Alone 91

Chapter 13.
The Weight of Absences That Don't Heal 95

Chapter 14.
Faith and Empathy Toward Migrants:
A Call to Conscience 101

Final Reflection 109

Epilogue 117

Open Letter to México 121

Migrant Glossary... 123

Author's Note

This book was born from a deep desire to share the stories of those who, like me, have experienced firsthand the weight, the hope, the silences, and the struggles of migration. I wanted to write from the heart, from the inside out —not guided by outside opinions or news headlines— because it is almost always easier to judge what we see than to understand the love behind why people migrate.

In a time when migrants are dehumanized, pointed at, blamed, and criminalized, I felt an urgent need to tell these stories. These are real accounts, painful but full of strength and dignity. They are not written to inspire pity, but to cultivate empathy.

Much has been said, written, and debated about migrants. Statistics, headlines, political speeches, and laws have tried to define our existence. But rarely are we heard with heart. This book is not academic or legal. It is not a guide or a defense. It is a testimony —a collection of experiences, pain, nostalgia, struggle, love, resilience, and dignity.

Many do not understand why a person would cross a border without "doing it the legal way." But the truth does not fit neatly in one sentence. Those who have never migrated —especially some U.S. citizens— often hold misguided beliefs about us, especially Latinos. They assume we cross illegally because it is easier or because we are nearby, avoiding the legal process by choice. But that could not be more wrong.

Most of us cross out desperation, not rebellion. If there had been a legal path, we would have taken it. But for millions of Mexicans and Latin Americans, that path simply does not exist. Even getting a tourist visa is incredibly hard. A work visa? Nearly impossible. Since 1986, there has been no immigration reform to address our reality. We may be neighbors to this country, but that has not given us access —only stigma.

I want to share what it means to migrate when there is no other choice. To grow up between two cultures, to raise a family in the shadows, to say goodbye to loved ones and never return, to carry an intact love for one's homeland from afar. This book is for those who crossed visible and invisible borders in search of a better life —and for those who have never migrated but are willing to listen with empathy.

I also want to respectfully address the narrative that links migrants —especially undocumented ones, now labeled as "illegal aliens"— with violence, crime, or the fentanyl crisis. I grieve for every life lost, and every family torn apart by addiction or violence. Some migrants have committed serious crimes. But the darkness of the human soul has no nationality. Drugs, crime, and harm are not exclusive to any country or immigration status. To

14

judge millions by the actions of a few is both unfair and dangerous.

Fentanyl and its consequences are part of a larger issue rooted in trauma, lack of mental health care, and broken systems. Those who traffic it must be held accountable —no matter where they come from. But we cannot criminalize the whole community because of the actions of some.

Migrants like me have also suffered loss. We have also known injustice. And still we work, contribute, and build with quiet strength. We come seeking work, security, and dignity. Not to break laws, but to survive.

Though this book is rooted in the Latino migrant experience, I must also acknowledge that the history of this country cannot be told without honoring Native Americans —the original stewards of this land— and the African American community, whose ancestors were forcibly brought here in chains. To speak of migration and ignore that chapter would be unjust.

We do not come to invade. We come to survive. To live with dignity. To find a small piece of hope.

May this book be an invitation to see migrants not as a threat, but as a mirror —people who want the same things you do: Safety, rest, belonging, and an opportunity.

To you, my migrant sister or brother, I hope you find yourself in these pages. Your story, your voice, your truth. Thank you for reading. Thank you for listening.

Selene Partida

Introduction

Migration —A Journey of Endless Shades of Gray

When we talk about migration, we often do so in black and white terms: legal or illegal, good, or bad, heroes or criminals. But the truth is far more complex. Migration is a deep human act, full of contradictions, pain, hope, and resistance.

This book does not seek to give legal answers or justify suffering. Nor does it aim to romanticize hardship. It seeks to build bridges —between those of us who migrate and those who do not understand why. Between those who leave everything behind and those to whom never had.

This is a human story told from the inside, by those who have lived it.

That is why I begin with my own story. Before we analyze causes, laws, or statistics, I invite you to see through my eyes what it means to leave your country at thirteen, cross a border in fear, grow up in a foreign land, fight to belong, and still hold on to your love for the home you left behind.

Every chapter that follows comes from that experience —and from the stories I have lived, witnessed, and

carried with me through more than thirty years of colla-
borating with the migrant community. This book does not
contain every voice. But it amplifies many. It is my tribute
to all those lives —visible and invisible. To those who
arrived, those who were forced to return, and those who
died trying.

Thank you for opening these pages. May they bring
you closer to our story.

Chapter I.
The Crossing

The Border

I still remember that night. It was a chilly night. It was March 21, 1991: Spring Day, Benito Juarez Day, and the day we left Mexico, or rather, Toluca, State of Mexico, the city where I was born and the city I left to begin our journey north, toward the unknown. But it was also the day that marked a before and after in my life.

That night we went to the bus station because there was not enough money for a plane ticket to the border city of Tijuana. So, my mother —a woman of strong character, determined face, and brave spirit— got on that bus with her four children, determined to complete the family with my father, who was already in Chicago. Her reason: to keep her family united.

That is how our journey began, the repeated story of so many migrant families: children, mothers, wives, fathers who risk everything for family reunification.

After almost two days on the road, we arrived in Tijuana. A relative connected my mother with a "coyote" or "pollero." She paid for everything she could; for that, she had to sell all the few or many belongings we had to make this trip possible. I remember that even my bicycle, which I adored so much, had to be sold to pay the high price of this crossing to "the other side".

At 13, I did not fully understand what we were about to do, what was happening, or the magnitude of the journey that awaited us that night. I still remember that moment when we arrived at the famous border fence. I still remember how surprised I was to see people selling tamales, hot coffee, and cinnamon tea in the middle of the wall: the good Mexican who always finds a way to survive. And like a good Mexican, I thought at that moment: "We're already at the wall and practically on the other side, we've already crossed, we've already made it, and there are even vendors here". But I could not have been more wrong. It was just the antechamber, the hallway to the long journey; the farewell committee, because that night we would cross.

After several hours waiting for the most suitable moment to cross —which I learned at that moment was during the changing of the guard at midnight— they gave us the signal to start walking, although sleep and cold were already beginning to weigh on us. We were a small group: my mother, my older sister (14), my little brother (6), my little sister (5), and me, along with another family. We walked for hours, among bushes, desert, loose earth, and darkness.

After a couple of hours of walking on the path, we came to a crossing where they charged for passing over an improvised bridge that avoided getting our feet wet. Everything was uncertain, but we continued. Along the way, we encountered another group that was hiding in fear. They were crying, shaken and terrified. One of the men told us they had been robbed at gunpoint. Then almost in a whisper, the women shared that they had been raped by a group of men they called the "cholos". I saw my mother turn pale; the fear was visible on her face. The coyote advised us to look for a stick or stone to defend ourselves. I looked for a stick. I was afraid, did not understand much, was tired, cold, and very scared. But there was no turning back: the only option was to continue. Seeing my mother's face of fear at that moment marked me forever, because it was there, I understood the real risk we were running.

I also remember the moment when we heard: "Here comes the mosquito!". The "mosquito" was the immigration helicopter. "Hide!". We hid among the dry desert bushes. The coyote warned us: "Don't look up, because your eyes reflect the light". I had never felt such curiosity to look at the sky and, at the same time, so much fear. I closed my eyes tightly, hoping they would not discover us. I felt the helicopter above us, its overwhelming noise and its light sweeping the desert. But they did not see us. They passed by. Until this moment I am sure God covered us with his mantle.

When the helicopter left, we continued walking for hours. Finally, at dawn, we reached a road. It was a highway, with cars passing at high speed. We had to cross it to reach the city. It was like the "Frogger" video game, the real version: dodging cars, running with accelerated hearts and being full of fear.

On the other side, a small house waited for us. The instructions were clear: total silence. We entered without making noise and went into a dark room with a bed where we all felt exhausted and fell asleep.

At dawn hour, upon waking up, my mother and my younger siblings were no longer there. Only my older sister and me. We panicked. We were immediately told that, although we had already "crossed", the journey was not finished yet. Part of the plan was that the others would be taken by another vehicle, to be able to pass the next checkpoint or customs station.

My sister and I had to hide on the back floor of a car. There was no space. We crouched between the feet and the back seat, curled up, hidden. It was the most uncomfortable trip of my life. I felt like my back was breaking. It was three or four hours like that, as I remember (now I know it was the journey from Tijuana to California), until we arrived at a parking lot where, finally, we met up with my mom. We hugged. It was impossible not to cry, because we felt great relief.

I felt relief because I thought the nightmare was over, that we had already made it. But the reality is that it was just beginning.

That is how, at 13 years old, I became "mojada", "undocumented", without any authorization or decision over my life. Just a brave mother doing what she believed was right to keep her family united. From that day began a life between shadow and hope.

I did not choose to be "illegal". Did I come or was I brought? Well, I was still a child. I came for love, for my mother's faith, for the desire to be with my father, like the family we were in.

This story is not unique. It is the story of thousands who had no other option, of those who crossed a border seeking a better life.

For years I lived in silence, with fear and shame, without understanding or knowing why I could not "fix papers" like other people had managed to do. What many do not understand or know is that, for millions of people like me, at that time and even now, that legal path simply does not exist. It is not that we do not want to "do things right", it is that the system leaves us out from the beginning.

This chapter does not seek to justify. It seeks to humanize. My hope is you, the reader —who perhaps has never lived something like this— to understand what it means to grow up in a country where you don't exist on paper, but you do in the farms, in the factories, in the kitchens, in the hotels, in the fields, and in the homes. Where your dreams stumble against invisible walls and your achievements is not always recognized.

My story did not begin at the border. It began much earlier, in Toluca, and continues today, with every step I take, with the certainty that no law, no document, can erase the dignity with which we have fought for a better life.

Chapter II.
Two Worlds

La Villita

Having the opportunity to gain experience up between two cultures, in two countries, in two vastly different worlds, can be a profoundly enriching experience. You learn, adapt, take the best from each one, and your view and perspective on life opens.

I am grateful to have lived that experience, but I also recognize that not everything is learning and cultural richness.

Growing up between two worlds also means that in one you do not fully belong... and in the other you are no longer physically present.

In one, they tell you that you are not from here. In the other, you have left, although your heart stayed there.

That is the dilemma.

You are in a country where you were not born, but you live, work, study, and adapt. However, you are not in the country you belong to by blood, history, language... because there was no security, stability, resources, or a clear future for you or your family.

I clearly remember when we arrived in Chicago, in the famous Mexican neighborhood known as *La Villita*, on the south side of the city. I was 13 years old. It was April 1991. At that age I did not understand much about politics, but

I did understand that there was a significant difference between those who could cross with a visa and those who could not.

I still did not grasp what it meant to live undocumented.

We entered high school—and it was a radical change. Although I had already heard English in movies and on television, I did not understand it or speak it. The only thing I knew was the classic stuff they teach in Mexico's public schools:

Pollito - Chicken
Ventana - Window
Puerta - Door
Pluma - Pen

Just a few of the first English words many of us learned as children.

All of us who have had to learn a new language out of necessity know what it is like

The Same the Fear, the nervousness of saying a word wrong, the lack of time and, at the same time, the need to learn quickly to be able to advance.

I also studied with books that had pronunciation in Spanish, for example:

"People - *pi puhl* - gente"
"To use - *tu yuuz* - usar"

I bought courses to learn English, attended classes, wrote phrases on sheets to memorize. I thought that would be my biggest challenge, but reality was even more complex.

Adapting to school was quite an odyssey. Violence and gangs at that time were also present: fights that broke out between Latinos and Black Americans, flying chairs, metal detectors when entering school, people shouting, graffiti, and more. It was a big cultural shock what I experienced the first months in school.

But the hardest thing was living that constant feeling of not fully belonging.

Let me tell you a bit more about me: I am the second of four children of my parents.

My dad, Eduardo Partida, a proud Michoacán native —whom I will talk about in other parts of the book— dreamed of returning to Mexico.

He said he wanted to wake up there, with the sounds of the town, the birds, the warmth of his Mexico.

That dream he did not fulfill in life... but he did in his eternal rest. I took him to rest forever in the land that he loved –San José de Gracia, Michoacán.

My older sister and I are only a year apart, so we entered the same high school grade together. That helped us because we accompanied each other.

She was fourteen, almost fifteen, when we migrated. A difficult age to leave friends, school, adolescence, just when you start to belong, to identify yourself. It is so difficult that I have known stories of young people who could not adapt, who suffer from deep depression, and sometimes make decisions as tragic as suicide.

Once settled, my sister and I decided to look for part-time work. It was common among students to work after school.

We went to the Discount Mall, a type of market inside a large warehouse where spaces were rented to sell merchandise (Flea market).

In that place I realized something that impacted me, and that still happens: observing how some immigrants take advantage of other immigrants.

Most of the owners of these stalls were also migrants, but even so they offered low wages, difficult conditions, and long work hours.

I say this with respect, but also with truth: we must become aware.

Among migrants we should not exploit each other but support each other. We have much in common: the same origin of struggle, the same dream of living better.

We also tried to apply at a fast-food restaurant. However, when we arrived, they asked us for the famous "mica," (a colloquial term migrants use to refer to the permanent resident card or any form of ID, including at times, forged papers obtained out of necessity) the social security number... documents we didn't have. That was the first time I understood that, although I was here, I did not fully belong.

It was hard to understand that we did not have either of the two basic things needed to get that job: neither a mica, nor a social security number.

The alternative for many was to look for jobs where they did not ask for it, but that paid much less. It was like living between the lines: in a world where I made an effort but was not legally visible.

That is when many people make desperate decisions: buy a fake mica, get a fake social security number, just to work, to survive.

Those decisions are not born from desire, but from desperation. No one makes decisions for pleasure; they are made from sheer need.

It is not about breaking rules, in some cases it is about staying alive. It is not a rebellion −it is survival.

Alongside all this, we heard in the news how some politicians point to us as a threat. They accuse us of being criminals, of bringing problems, of damaging this country.

However, they do not talk about the migrant who packs bread in a bakery, who takes care of children, who cleans their houses, who delivers food, who builds buildings and fixes their houses.

They do not talk about the migrant who lives in silence, who works hard, who respects the rules, even though they are living in the shadows.

As I mentioned at the beginning of this section, living between two cultures has wonderful aspects: becoming bilingual, understanding two realities, expanding your vision of the world. The United States is a country rich in cultures, stories, and diversity.

But that richness also contrasts with the harsh experience of those who —like me— grew up between two worlds without fully belonging to either.

Today, decades later, that same duality persists.

We migrants have become political pawns on a large chess board. We are mentioned in speeches, in campaigns, in newscasts...

I remember recently seeing a press conference by a governor in the United States who said —without hesitation— that undocumented people are a threat to the country.

That immigration raids were "necessary" to keep the population safe.

He said that illegal migrants —"illegal aliens"— caused accidents, committed abuse, were thieves, sold drugs, drove drunk, caused violence and many other crimes.

Although I do not deny reality. Sadly, there have been cases where undocumented migrant people have committed such crimes. Painful, terrible cases, and there is no excuse for those actions.

They hurt us.

They shame us.

And we pray for the victims and their families.

But what also hurts is that they try to hold an entire community responsible, as if evil only lived in migrants.

That is dishonest.

Because evil has no passport.

Darkness and light exist in all humanity.

Good and evil, compassion and violence... are part of human history, from long before borders or visas existed.

Yes, we must eradicate violence.
Yes, we must combat abuse and crime.

But we will not do it if we continue pointing to migrants as scapegoats.

What I do know is that as migrants we are grateful: grateful for the country that saw us born, for our roots, for our culture, for our customs...

But also grateful to this country that gives us opportunities, feeds us, gives us work, and allows us to be a community.

Although today we continue fighting to be recognized, we hope one day to be able to belong to both. That is the paradox of growing up between two worlds.

You are in one, grateful, building a life.
But you still feel your soul belongs to the other.

And meanwhile, you strive to fit in, to create a bridge, to find a home that can exist between both lands.

And so, we began to live between two worlds...

Learning to navigate the obstacles of one,
While carrying the pain of the other.

Chapter III.
Between Shadow and Hope

The Paper Doors

Arriving in the United States did not mean arriving in paradise. It meant starting a new life... in the shadows. From that moment I became an "illegal" person, a word I never fully understood, because I did not feel illegal. I felt like a girl wanting to be with her family, study, enjoy, get ahead... although the law did not see it that way.

As I shared earlier in this book, when I graduated from high school, I found myself facing closed doors. It was not for lack of talent, effort, or dedication. It was simply because I did not have the documents. The opportunities did not exist for me; they were not within my reach.

Those doors, opportunities that open easily for so many, for me were sealed.

I baptized them, I called them "the paper doors", because a simple paper could open them... or keep them closed.

After applying to a couple of colleges and finally being able to attend one briefly —but which I had to abandon when for the third time they asked me for my social security number, which I didn't have— out of fear, out of shame, I had to leave school.

I also tried to join the Navy, the Army, hoping to serve and open a path. But that was not possible for me either. I lacked that magic paper that decided my destiny.

At that time, I was highly active in the local Catholic church, in the youth group. There I discovered how beautiful it was to serve others. The nuns who attended Saint Agnes church, in La Villita, had a mission house in Ciudad Obregón, Sonora. I deeply admired their dedication, how they gave themselves to the community, how they cared for and loved everyone.

That is how, when I turned eighteen, I made the difficult decision to return to Mexico to enter that convent. I could not advance in this country, but maybe I could serve in mine. I said goodbye to my mother, my father, and with faith in God I left, with the hope of returning to Mexico to serve my country. I told my parents: if God wants me to return to the United States, He will open the way.

I arrived in Ciudad Obregón, Sonora, without knowing anyone. In the convent I met other young women, including one who also came from Chicago. They were months of formation, dedication, and learning. I learned more about Mexico, its cultures, its traditions, and the unconditional love that so many of those religious sisters gave with humility.

But I also discovered the other side of religion —not of faith since faith and religion are two quite different things. I learned that, even in holy places, where service is supposed to reign, there can be pride, ego, narcissism.

My experience in two worlds gave me the courage to question injustice. I asked why some sisters had to serve as servants to priests, fathers, and seminarians, who often did not serve their people, much less their missions in the middle of the desert, where people thirst for the living water we preached. I questioned the power and lack of dedication. That audacity cost me my permanence in the convent.

My love for Jesus's message remains intact. Even so, I understood that sometimes the problem is not the message, but the messengers.

I found myself back in Chicago. It was literally God's hand that allowed my return. I entered accompanied by a nun and, although we went through customs, they did not ask me for my documents (which I did not have). I got on a bus bound for Chicago. However, my inner voice told me: "Don't sit in front or back, sit in the middle". I did so. I listened to my sixth sense.

Two hours later, immigration agents stopped the bus. They took down the first three passengers for not having documents. That is how I was able to continue the trip to Chicago.

Shortly after, I met a neighbor who invited me to his church. He was a handsome, kind man, full of faith. He talked to me about God and forming a family. He was seeking me out increasingly, so I decided to be honest. I told him I was undocumented and that I would probably return to Mexico, because I did not see a future here.

He had a certain interest in me. He asked me not to leave, to give him a chance to get to know each other. He told me he wanted to help me with my immigration situation and form a family serving God.

I was 19 years old. I want to continue to be —an idealist, wanting to serve and with the desire to please my mother, to form a family and not have to leave Chicago again. I thought it was the best decision I could make. I let myself be carried away by the moment, the need, the emotions.

We married very soon, without getting to know each other well, and I without knowing much about his past... or the demons he carried.

The wedding night was my first encounter with domestic violence.

That is how this dysfunctional cycle began: abuse, forgiveness, promises, honeymoon... and again the abuse.

I decided to stay because I had made a promise: "until death do us part" (old school ideas). I had my first child very quickly and soon after I was expecting the second. I knew it was not a healthy relationship, but when I tried to leave, I was already trapped, not only by fear, but by threats.

—"If you leave, I'll call immigration".

—"If you leave me, I'll report your parents to immigration since they are undocumented".

Words hurt as much as blows. The reproaches were constant:

—"You only married me for the papers."

Even after 13 years of marriage and three children, those words did not stop. It was through this marriage that I regularized my immigration status. I asked for forgiveness before the law, paid the fines, and complied with every step to regularize my status.

However, nothing cures emotional pain. It took me years to heal, find the strength to leave, and understand that my freedom should never depend on a document, on threats... or on a toxic relationship.

I share this not to inspire pity, but to give voice to those who have lived something similar.

Many migrant people —for love or hope— have ended up in relationships where immigration status becomes a weapon, an emotional prison, another shadow. To them I encourage you: you are not alone. There is life beyond fear.

A mica, a green card, should never be worth more than your dignity, your mental health, and your freedom.

I share part of my story as a migrant, how I came to this country and some of the challenges and tribulations I had to face. I do it with humility and from the heart because it is precisely through these experiences —sometimes hard, others full of hope— that a deep love, respect, and admiration for the migrant community was born in me.

Because I am one of them. Because I have walked those paths. Because I have lived that cycle.

This book is born from that place: from the genuine desire for our voice to be heard, not as figures or stereotypes, but as human beings with history, with dreams, with wounds, with contributions.

I invite you to continue reading, to continue walking with me through this journey of migrants.

I was encouraged by a few people who are very close to me to tell my story, not because it is unique, but because it reflects many others. To be able to understand that not all cases are the same, that not all routes are the same, that not all arrivals have the same form.

Chapter IV.
Forced Migration

Out of Necessity

Some of us arrived as children, others by our own decision. Many, as you will see in this chapter, arrive out of necessity, danger, or desperation.

That is what we call forced migration, and that is what we will talk about next.

The stories of those who leave their home do not begin at the border or the moment they set foot in another country. They start much earlier: in the streets where they grew up, in the decisions their parents made, in moments of uncertainty where fear and hope intertwined.

Forced migration is not just a geographical journey, but an emotional one.

It is grief for what is left behind and anxiety for what is to come.

Some people flee from violence, from governments that do not offer them security or a future. Others, from extreme poverty, from lack of opportunities, from a system that marginalizes them and condemns them to a life of deprivation.

Likewise, there are those who migrate because climate change has destroyed their lands, because water stopped flowing in their rivers, because their crops died before bearing fruit.

Forced migration is the echo of many injustices, but also proof of an unbreakable will to survive.

María and the Burden of Migration

Some time ago, I had to work in Ohio. In the hotel where I stayed, I was able to make friends with the people who worked there, cleaning rooms and in the food area. I have always felt that among migrants there is an immediate connection; it is enough to start a conversation to know their common stories.

That is how I met María. She was in her thirties and, as usually happens among us migrants, our chat began with the classic question: "Where are you from?". "From Tenancingo, State of Mexico," she answered with a shy smile.

The next question was inevitable:

"How long have you been here?".

"Two years now," she said, as if she still could not quite believe it.

As the days passed, trust grew. One afternoon, after several chats in the hotel hallways, she asked me quietly: "Do you know any number to report someone who sells drugs... but anonymously?".

Her question took me by surprise. My curiosity grew and I asked her why she needed it. María sighed, looked around, as if making sure no one else was listening, and finally told me her story.

48

She had come to the United States with her fifteen-year-old son. She worked all day at the hotel and, on weekends, if there was an opportunity, washed dishes at a restaurant. Her son went to school but spent many hours alone at home. Over time, he had made friends with some people at a beauty salon near where they lived. María feared they were selling drugs and that they were influencing her son.

I asked her why she had made the decision to migrate and if he was her only child. "No... I have another one, three years old".

Her eyes filled with tears as she said it. She explained that in Mexico she worked in a factory, but it closed, and she could not find another job. What little she earned was not enough to support her children and help her parents, who were already elderly. Her husband had abandoned her and, without much education.

Since she could not finish more than elementary school —she did not have many options. Migrating was the only way out she found to try to give them a better life.

"Why didn't you bring your little son?" I asked cautiously.

"I could only bring the older one...".

She lowered her gaze and stayed silent for a few seconds before continuing.

"It hurt me a lot to leave him with my parents, but I had no other choice".

That is the problem with forced migration: family separation. Families are left fragmented. Sometimes it is the father or mother who leaves, leaving their children behind. In other cases, they manage to emigrate with one but must leave others in their country of origin. María, like many other migrant mothers, faced a double absence: her little son on the other side of the border, growing up without her; and her teenage son, here, exposed to dangers while she worked tirelessly.

I did mental calculations: If María worked 35 hours a week at the hotel and earned US$14 per hour, after a forced lunch hour without pay, that meant before taxes she earned around US$500 a week. After deductions, she had about US$1,500 a month. With cheap rent of US$800, transportation, food, and other expenses, maybe she managed to send about US$300 a month to Mexico. US$300 dollars to support her little son and her parents.

Forced migration is an open wound. María did not leave because she wanted to, but because she had no other choice. Despite that, even after crossing the border, the difficulties do not end. Here, far from her homeland, her struggle is just beginning.

Chapter V.
Modern Slavery

The Price of Silence

Recently, I had the opportunity to work in response to hurricanes Milton and Helene, in the state of Florida. From the first day I realized something that marked me: especially in the affected areas near the beach —where the tourism industry is the economic engine— there was an impressive presence of people from Chiapas and Guatemala.

Many of them did not speak Spanish as their native language. They spoke Tzotzil, Tzeltal, K'iche', Maya and other Indigenous languages. I was moved by their resilience… but also by the pain of knowing that my beloved Mexico —Guatemala, and Central America— are losing their valuable people.

My thought was clear: Mexico is bleeding its people, its culture.

I have the audacity to feel, to think that my Mexico is selling, renting, or letting go of its people, and its Indigenous people. People who should be cultural treasures, living pillars of our history, are now picking strawberries under the Florida sun, working exhausting shifts to sustain the economy of a country that does not even recognize them, to which they do not belong.

Among them I met Elia. Her mobile home had been severely damaged by the hurricane Milton. Water had entered and the little they had was ruined. Despite this, she was seeking help with dignity, without complaining. Over time, I was able to sit and chat with her. I asked her what made her leave Chiapas and come north.

Her gaze hardened.

"My mom died when I was about twelve or thirteen", she told me. "No one helped me. I slept on the street and sold crafts to survive".

She told me about the streets of San Cristóbal, of Tuxtla, of those colorful stalls that we all look at, but few value. As a child, she sold her people's tradition, their art, while sleeping on sidewalks.

One day, someone from the town was organizing a trip to the United States. One of her brothers told her: "This could be your way out". And so, it was.

At barely fourteen years old, she began her journey. She crossed the border and started working in the California fields, picking oranges. There she met another migrant, whom she married noticeably young. At 19 she already had two children. They moved to Georgia, and then to Florida, looking for work.

"What do you do now?" I asked her.

"I'm strawberry picking".

She explained that, when there are many strawberries, they pay her two dollars for each box with eight small baskets. In one hour, she can pick between six and eight boxes... if there's abundance. If not, three or four.

Despite the demanding work and her damaged house, Elia was a strong, kind woman, full of light. While we talked, her husband tried to repair what remained of the mobile home. Before saying goodbye, she told me something I still carry in my heart:

"The problem isn't so much the work... It is water. When we pick strawberries, although we use boots and gloves, water gets in, and that water has pesticides and chemicals. And now, in the community clinic, there are many people with cancer. I don't know if that's the reason... but that's what most of us who pick strawberries think".

I asked her to record a small video to show how migrants live. She agreed. I wanted the world to see her face, her voice, her truth. Although, when I uploaded it to social media, the judgment was immediate and cruel.

Instead of listening to her story, people commented about her appearance, her age, the disorder of her mobile home. They mocked an old truck that appeared in the background:

"Suffering? But look what truck she has".

They did not understand —or did not want to observe— that they had just survived a hurricane, and that the truck was not a luxury, it was a work tool. That it was not disorder, it was survival. That her face was not mistreated or cared for with expensive moisturizers, it was the reflection of years of effort and hard labor.

I call this modern slavery.

The same slavery lived by those who worked in milk barns in Minnesota, in chicken factories, in watermelons, tomato, carrot fields, in packing plants, in greenhouses, in meat plants.

While they work for pennies, remittances become Mexico's highest source of income, surpassing even tourism and the automotive industry. It pains me to say it, but we export our own people —compatriots— to the north... in exchange for dollars.

That, too, must said.

Because they are essential workers. They, too, deserve recognition, respect, and visibility.

They should appear in newscasts, in campaigns, in history books. Because thanks to them, there's milk on the table, fruit in the market, flowers on altars.

Elia and her husband are undocumented. They live at the mercy of an immigration policy that offers them no out. They form part of a binational family: children born in the United States, parents without papers, without a clear path toward immigration reform.

Despite that, they continue working. In silence. Invisible. But essential.

Chapter VI.
Return Migration

Going Back

Migration return: a path full of nostalgia, fear and hope

Another great chapter we must tell is that of return migration. There are many people who live in fear of this possibility, especially those who have been living abroad for years —or even decades. The country where they reside has become their home, their new house. They have settled, have family, children, and some, with much effort, have managed to buy property or start a business. They have learned to live day by day in their new country, creating their little Mexico far from Mexico, living with constant nostalgia for the real Mexico.

Since 1986, when the last amnesty occurred, almost 40 years have passed. There are companions who have waited all this time for a new opportunity, dreaming of the possibility of returning to Mexico. And, of course, there are the brave ones who have tried it, crossing the cruel border repeatedly.

For those who have been living for 30, 20, 15, 10 or even just 5 years in a country with new roots and a new family, the idea of being forced to return becomes a nightmare. It is not a lack of love for the homeland, but the most beautiful and valuable thing in life —family, friends, house, work— is now in the "wrong place".

Life becomes confusing, uncertain, with very few possibilities of returning without losing everything. Nostalgia for families in Mexico —parents, siblings, cousins— gradually calms when a new life is built. But when the threat of deportation or forced migration arrives, everything achieved is left behind.

I still remember the phone call I received from a man from the State of Mexico, whom I did not know, but who called me seeking support. Let us call him Juan.

Juan told me he had lived in Detroit, Michigan, for almost 25 years. That, like several of us, he had crossed the border, was undocumented, and therefore drove without a license. Out of necessity, he decided to buy a false identity.

"He did not want to break the law by buying a false identification" he told me, "But out of necessity, to want to work and support my family".

Something that the law, when it is rigid and does not understand human context, cannot see.

One day, returning from work, the sheriff stopped him because one of his taillights would not turn on. As routine, they asked for his driver's license. He showed the only one he had: the fake license.

The sheriffs, realizing this, arrested him and gave him five years' sentence in an immigration detention center. He told me he served three years and then they deported him to Mexico.

The call he made to me from Mexico was heart-breaking. Hearing a man cry while telling me that his wife, his children, his grandchildren, his house, and his life were there... and that he, here, in Mexico, had nothing.

Not even his birth certificate.

He asked me:

"How do I start over?".

These are untold testimonies. Stories of pain, of invisible losses. The cruelty, sorrow, and sadness of forced migration without a plan, without support.

On the other hand, even those who plan to voluntarily return to their beloved Mexico face enormous challenges. The more time you spend abroad, the harder it is to adapt. Recovering your documents, processing your voter ID, remaking your legal identity... Especially if your children were born abroad. They also face culture shock. It is getting a job, a house. It is starting over.

That is why it is important to understand the phenomenon of return migration from a humanitarian point of view, with empathy. We return because we miss, because we carry nostalgia inside. We miss the smells, colors, flavors of Mexico. The holidays, family gatherings. We return with the hope that our Mexico embraces us, understands us, and helps us start again.

Hoping that return does not feel like defeat, but like the beginning of a new story.

Where the pain and scars of having lived far away are transformed into wonderful experiences, into strength, into a breath of life that is never forgotten.

Chapter VII.
Binational Families

Different Ways of Growing

Unfortunately, sometimes it is easier to jump to conclusions or judge without understanding.

In 2023, a regional Mexican music group, formed by young people of a Michoacán family but born in Washington state —a place with a large Latino population— visited Mexico. During their visit, they were harshly criticized for expressing that they did not really like Mexican food and preferred, in quotes, "chicken nuggets". They also commented that they did not like Mexico that much. The media destroyed them mercilessly, without stopping to understand their position.

For those of us who have children born in the United States —or in another country— this is easy to understand. Often, the famous chicken nuggets and other similar foods are part of their daily life, especially in families where both parents work long hours in factories or in the field. That fast and accessible food becomes habitual: it is cheap, easy, and part of their environment. In Mexico, their equivalent could be a torta or some tacos from the market.

Another point few understood is that these young people grew up in an environment quite different from Mexico City or any town in Michoacán. They are a second generation, which means that love for Mexico, language and traditions was transmitted to them by their parents, because they themselves have not yet lived them, have not experienced them, have not discovered them first-hand.

Seeing how they were treated, without giving them the opportunity to fall in love with Mexico, was sad. No one stopped to think about where they came from or where they really lived, what their environment was. They were not given empathy. They were not given the opportunity to know and understand their roots before judging them.

I wanted to tell this example because I know that today, and in years to come, many binational families will return to Mexico with their children born in the United States or other countries. And likewise, they are going to face these same situations: mockery, criticism, or judgment at school, in their neighborhood, or even among family and friends. There will be those who criticize or judge them without understanding the complexity of their identity.

They do not understand that children and young people exist in two cultures, two worlds, trying to coexist in one heart.

Through this example, to whoever is reading this, I ask that they show more kindness. That they remember the Mexican hospitality that makes us so proud. That, instead of mocking or pointing, they help this new generation of Mexicans born abroad to fall in love with their culture, our gastronomy, our traditions, our country. Only then will they be able to feel part of the land that also belongs to them, although they were born far from it.

Chapter VIII.
Citizen Children, Undocumented Parents

Citizen Children, Undocumented Parents

What a strong and real phrase: "Citizen children, un-documented parents".

A phrase that represents the life of so many of us who, after arriving in this country without papers, followed life's natural law: we fell in love, formed a family... and our children were born here.

For many, that moment was a cause for joy. We felt that, somehow, they had already "made it".

That, being citizens, they would have everything we have not been able to achieve security, rights, opportunities. We felt, deep in our hearts, that we gave them a great gift. That their nationality is a kind of shield, a door that we were never able to cross. We gave them something that many others —have not been able to obtain: legal belonging.

And although we live in the shadows, there is a small pride that sustains us: knowing that, at least with them, we did something right. It comforts our hearts to think they will have a better future. One that is not full of fear of being discovered, detained, deported.

In the beginning of 2025, I was in California, just during the marches against the new administration's immigration policies. There I saw crowd of young people with signs held high. One of them, large, red, remained etched in my memory:

"My grandma is not a criminal".

Another said:

"Thank you to my parents, because they gave me everything when they had nothing". They were not isolated phrases. They were cries of love.

Reading those banners filled me with joy, pride, and hope. Seeing that new generation —citizen children of migrant parents— understanding what we have given and what we have lost, was a balm for the soul.

Because it is true: many of us did not have —nor do we have— anything, but even so we have tried to give everything.

And that phrase: "My grandma is not a criminal", touched my heart.

Because, although now they want to label us as "illegals," the question still hurts:

What does it mean to be illegal?

Can a human being be illegal?

The answer is no.

What is missing is not dignity, it is a document.

I remember when I finished high school. I wanted to continue studying and get a better job. But I did not have what this country demanded: a social security number, a residence card. For me, they were just papers... but without them, The Paper Doors were closed.

I felt like I was in front of a great buffet. I could see it, I could smell it, but I could not touch it. And I, hungry, eager, with dreams... could not access anything.

That is the impotence we feel.

The frustration of living in a society where a person's value is measured by a paper. And yes, laws exist. Documents exist. They have a purpose.

They help us organize and coexist.

But when those laws stop serving people and start destroying dreams, families, futures, loves and opportunities... then we have lost our way.

The day we understand that documents should work for people —and not the other way around— that day we will have taken a great step as a society.

Chapter IX.
Daily Uncertainty

The Real Uncertainty: Fear of the Void That Can Open at Any Moment Under Our Feet

Living as an undocumented person in a foreign country is living under daily uncertainty. This uncertainty can present itself in many forms: fear that, suddenly, at your job, the boss, company, or agency will verify your immigration status; that they will check the Social Security number you are working with. It's the constant fear of driving and being stopped by police, whether for a vehicle plate failure, a simple traffic control or, worse yet, because you don't have a driver's license —something that, in many states, is difficult to obtain if you're undocumented.

Although we live grateful for each day and make plans like any other person, in an undocumented person's mind that question always dwells: what would happen if they detain me?, what would happen if at my job they check my papers? what will happen if they deport me from one moment to another?

The problem is not just returning to the country of origin. The real pain is in everything that would be left behind: family, children born here, belongings, acquired commitments, the community we have helped build. What would happen to the life that, with so much effort, we built here, that we learned to organize, create, design?

That is the real uncertainty: fear of the void that can open at any moment under our feet.

I understand that everyone, somehow, lives with uncertainty about the future —even those who never emigrated. In contrast, for an undocumented person, that uncertainty carries a double or triple burden. It's not just about an uncertain future; it's that your entire life built in another country can disappear in a matter of hours —or minutes, in some cases— for something as simple as an administrative verification, a court or lack of a document, the Paper doors will never open and in some cases they will close forever.

Especially in these times of hardening immigration policies, this shadow is even heavier.

For those who read this book, I want to invite you to reflect on that extra layer of uncertainty with which many migrants without documents —and in some cases, with documents— live each day. Despite this, we continue dreaming, we continue faithfully sending money to our families, we continue fighting to create something better. However, we live as if we had a thorn stuck in our soul, with that painful question: what if they discover me? What if everything disappears? What if they deport me?

That thorn, moreover, is loaded with shame, fear, and pain. It is difficult to explain. Even so, for those of us who have had to fill out a form, an application, look for employment or simply face the question: "Do you have a Social Security number?", we know that wound opens again. It is a silent wound, but always present.

76

Chapter X.
30 and 40 Years Without Documents: The Human Cost of Migratory Limbo

Living in Limbo

A few days ago, I saw an image on social media: a man, already older, maybe in his sixties, with a tired face and deep gaze, as if reflecting on his life. Above, there was a written phrase: "I'm just going three years to the States and coming back...".

And in quotes, like a bitter joke: "Thirty years later". That is the story of so many...

Many of us came to this country with the idea of staying a couple of years, making some dollars, saving for a house, a taxi, a store, etc.

We were just going to "study English".
It would just be two or three years.
It was just a visit.

But those years became ten...
Then twenty...
Then thirty or forty...
And we continue in migratory limbo.

A limbo that, as its name says, is not solid ground, is not a safe place or of belonging. It is between two worlds: one that does not give us documents, benefits or recognize us, and another that no longer waits for us.

Each year we live with that hope. Every time a new administration enters, we think that maybe, now yes, there will be an immigration reform, amnesty, a permit, a law that recognizes us.

Maybe this year, this congress, this president... However, we continue waiting, with faith in God... and with hope placed in some public servant taking pity on us.

Meanwhile, we continue planting here. We invest our years, our strength, our life, although the only thing we long for is that: that one day someone recognizes us as part of this great nation.

"We accept you; you've earned it, you can stay and live in peace".

We want that symbolic document that recognizes our existence, our contribution, our effort, our time. Because this is not just time or investment, it is the only life we have.

The hardest part is the other face of limbo: nostalgia for a country you have not seen for 10, 15, 30 years.

A country you cannot return to, not because you do not want to, but because you do not have the documents to do so without losing everything.

There is no return date.

There is no return ticket.

Just another Paper Door.

And if you go back... what if next year the reform comes?

What if just when you leave, it was finally your turn? What if they finally make an immigration reform? That eternal doubt... is also part of limbo.

In conversations among migrants, it is inevitable many times to have this conversation:

"Where are you from?"

"How long have you been here?"

"I have 10 years..."

"I have 20..."

"I've been here since '86 since the last amnesty".

Yes, 1986. The last time a large number of people were legally recognized was almost four decades ago. In some cases, it can be seen or felt like a forty-year sentence.

A sentence that took us away from our families, which took away the possibility of returning, which made us live between hope and fear. Sometimes we silently envy those who can come and go.

Honestly, I also came to feel that.

On my social media, on more than one occasion I have published photos when I have been in Mexico, when I have gone for work, activism, some family event, or commitment with migrants.

On more than one occasion, some followers have written to me:

"You yes, Selene, because you can. You do have papers. You can go to Mexico and return". "I have been more than 20 years without seeing my mom".

"For you it's very easy to travel and speak".

At first, I tried to explain to them. I told them: "I was also there. I also spent years without being able to go. I understand you. I am doing this precisely to make visible what we migrants live in".

But they answered me the same:

"It's very easy for you to say, because you can".

Eventually I understood what their comments shared with me. I understood that, sometimes, when pain and impotence are so great, not even the best explanation consoles.

It is not envy, nor jealousy, it is deep desperation. That is The Paper Door. It is that pain or impotence of having the money, time, desire... but not the document. That is limbo, which is a silent sentence.

If you who are reading this are a migrant, maybe you can understand what I am referring to or know what I am talking about.

And if you are not a migrant and are trying to understand us, I invite you to imagine:

Maybe you have everything to return to your country and visit your family —which you haven't seen for years—, you have everything you have to make that trip... except that document that will allow you to return to your current life in this country, if that's your plan.

A document that defines whether you can hug your mother, see your father alive or be at your brother's funeral.

That is the human cost of migratory limbo: The Paper Door that places us in a position of invisibility and vulnerability.

Living without papers or documents is like having one foot inside and another outside. It is hiding a part of our identity for fear of being discovered. It is scary that, at work, at our children's school or at any daily interaction, someone discovers our condition and that changes everything.

For those who have not experienced this experience, it can be difficult to understand. It is like waiting for a sunny day that never comes; it is always cloudy, always under the shadow of that gray cloud.

Although we live in a world with innovative technologies, with medical advances and new treaties, millions of people still continue living in shadows due to our migratory situation.

Yes, we are supposed to learn from history to not repeat the same mistakes and grow as human beings. Maybe I dare too much in wanting to compare, even minimally, what undocumented migrants live with what our Jewish brothers and sisters experienced during World War II (I write this minimal comparison with much respect to the Jewish people).

At that time, for the simple fact of being Jewish and not fitting the Nazi ideal, thousands of people had to live in the shadows, hiding to survive. Although circumstances are different, the sensation of being invisible and fearing for our security is a constant feeling.

Maybe my comparison sounds dramatic, but for someone who has lived in shadow for years, hoping that a public servant, senator, congressman, congresswoman or government administration takes pity and grants amnesty, a permit, a card, or Social Security number, that is the hope millions live with.

We have hope placed in God, in the Creator, in the owner of "of course yes!", but we also have hope that man recognizes our humanity and gives us the opportunity to come out of the shadows.

Chapter XI.
When Death Comes Far Away

When Death Finds You Far from Home

Death is, perhaps, the only certainty we have from the moment we are born. We could talk about it from many angles, but today I want to talk to you about a different death: the one that finds us far away.

When death comes far —far from home, from town, from family, from land— pain becomes different. If you are a migrant, surely you already know what I am referring to.

And if you are not but are reading this book with genuine desire to understand us from a very humanitarian point of view, I thank you.

Because this is also part of our narrative: dying in foreign land.

Sadly, it has not been one, nor two, nor three times that I have received calls, messages, requests... all with a common urgency: helping to return the body of a migrant brother or sister who died far from home, because they stopped breathing in this country, far from their children, far from their wife, their parents, far from their own, far from their town.

Many relatives don't know where to start, don't have resources, and the only way to find comfort is to be able to say goodbye, even if it's just that: see them and say goodbye one last time, in a dignified way, full of love among their own.

In other words, mourn their dead. That also means when death comes far away. It comes far from the dream that made us leave home, far from the idea of coming to work for a few years to save something and return, far from that promise that broke without warning.

When death comes far away, another face of the migrant also surfaces: their kind hearts. The community reacts with resilience, with generosity, with empathy, with love. We make collections, organize fundraisers, ask for help, knock on doors, ask for favors, make calls...

All to send our migrant brother or sister back home, even if it is in a coffin. Even if it is just so their mother, father, wife, children, or friends can have that comfort and can sigh for them.

But there is another way death also comes far away: when it takes us on the road.

Just like those who die at the border, on the road, in the desert, in the river, in that attempt to achieve something better...

Those left in oblivion, drowned in a crossing, or abandoned by traffickers who commercialize with the most sacred: life.

When the migrant becomes a number.

A dollar.

A bundle in a trailer.

Where death comes among strangers, who become travel and wake companions.

Without air.
Without water.
Without a name.

When it comes nameless, bodiless, without explanation, and it leaves a family waiting for a call... some news... a sign of life.

It also comes far away like this, when it occurs in an accident fleeing from fear of police or immigration, or when it occurs by an act of injustice, by hands of those who believe themselves law, but are only men empowered by their weapons and a lack of love for their neighbor.

One of the saddest things that can happen to us as migrants is this: dying far away, without being able to close the cycle with our family, without farewell, without return. That is also part of our story.

That is... when death comes far away.

Chapter XII.
The Silent Grief
We Carry Alone

Without the Final Farewell

When I speak of migrant stories of those who could not say goodbye, I am not referring to one or two... there are many, too many.

So many, they hurt just remembering them. Stories of those who never saw their loved ones again.

Stories perhaps like mine: I still remember, I was 13 years old, the last time I saw my grandparents in my beloved Mexico. We were heading to the bus terminal, on our way to Tijuana, where we crossed the border.

I did not know it then, but that would be the last time I would see my grandfather "Pepe" Estrada. His face is still etched in my mind, as if it were yesterday.

His thick mustache, the cigarette in his hand —that one he never left—, the brown fabric pants worn out and his figure leaning on the metal fence that surrounded the house.

He looked at me tenderly:

"Goodbye, little witch. Take care", as he used to call me jokingly–little witch, with that hoarse and loving voice. I responded with a smile, waving from the car window. That was the last image I have of him.

My last look, my last memory, my last goodbye... although I did not know it would be. That is the story of many of us.

We think we will only be away for a year or two, we make plans, we dream of returning. But life —and death— do not always consult us.

Chapter XIII.
The Weight of Absences That Don't Heal

The Internal Contradiction

Throughout the previous two chapters we have tried to share the migrant's pain when death comes far away, when the migrant cannot say goodbye to their loved ones, when they cannot close that grief cycle.

That is precisely what constitutes this part: absence does not heal. That pain many migrants carry like a constant thorn.

A thorn that sometimes transforms into anger, into deep sadness, into guilt... for not having been there, for having stayed, for having continued.

It is difficult to explain, but the migrants often do not fully understand how they are still far away.

How, without wanting it, due to life's circumstances, they stayed in another country while their family lived important moments: weddings, birthdays, graduations, illnesses, births... or farewells.

Despite that, one learns to conform with photos, with messages, with calls, with memories. But deep down, we know something left us forever, that we miss moments that will not return.

That is the absence that does not heal what we did not live.

What we could not share.
What could have been?
What will no longer be?

At the same time, an internal contradiction occurs to us.

Because if we returned, there would also be doubts:

What if I had stayed? What would have happened?

This is my theory: "The migrant's theory".

We live divided by the Paper Doors, between two worlds, spaces, moments, time: the physical, where we are today, working, building, creating... and the emotion where our memories, our loves, our roots, and part of our identity dwell. It is a double life.

And although time helps —yes, it helps— to accommodate pain, it does not always heal it. With time we forget some promises, some dates, some details.

What we never lived is never fully forgotten.

The hug you did not give.
The burial you could not attend.
The last conversation did not happen.

For those who have lost someone —a father, mother, brother, friend, partner, compadre— and could not say goodbye, they know exactly what I am talking about.

That is the other bill we pay as migrants:

The goodbye not given, the absence that stayed like a knot in the soul.

My invitation to my migrant brothers and sisters is this:
It is okay to feel, it is okay to cry, it is okay to talk.
It is okay to live with grief, work through it, honor it.
We are not made of steel, and we do not have to be.

And for those who read this from the outside, we do not ask for compassion, we do not ask you to feel pity, it is about you understanding a little more of the migrant's heart.

That heart that often does not speak, but continues beating strongly while working in silence, with gratitude and love.

Because, although we carry wounded souls, we continue giving the best of ourselves: when we cook in the restaurant where we work, when we pack in the factory, when we bake bread at dawn, when we cut grass under the sun, when we drive through the city doing Uber or deliveries, when we sell our food, when we clean offices and when we care for the elderly and children entrusted to us...

There also lives the migrant.
With their story, their pain, and their hope.

Chapter XIV.
Faith and Empathy Toward Migrants: A Call to Conscience

Understanding The True Message

It is impossible to talk about migration, humanism, and empathy without mentioning the Creator. In the Old Testament, we find in Deuteronomy 10:19 a clear mandate:

"And you shall love the foreigner, for you were foreigners in the land of Egypt".

This verse reminds us that God hears the pleas of foreigners and does not abandon them, because He himself understands what it is to be a stranger. This is precisely the purpose of this chapter: that we understand, like God, the challenges and journey of immigrants.

In the New Testament, Jesus teaches us in Matthew 25:35-40:

"For I was hungry, and you gave me food; I was thirsty, and you gave me drink; I was a stranger, and you welcomed me...

Truly, I say to you, as you did it to one of the least of these my brothers, you did it to me".

These words are a direct call to all those who consider themselves Christians and believers, but who, however, see migrants with contempt or annoyance.

It is understandable that there are challenges in border cities, especially in recent years, where a large number of migrants have arrived and, sometimes, have had to make the streets their home. However, in moments of frustration, it's essential to remember that there's a Supreme Being who understands immigration and the desire of these people —of us, migrants— to live in a place with peace and harmony, where we're allowed to work and our families have the same opportunities.

Often, on the road, frustration, desperation, and anxiety grow.

Uncertainty generates fear and, sometimes, triggers complaints and neglect, making understanding difficult between those affected and those who migrate. In those moments of desperation, I invite my migrant companions to remember the words of Jesus Christ and to keep in mind that, according to the Bible —God's word— He hears the foreigner's pleas.

New International Version (NIV) —Matthew 7:7-8:

"Ask and it will be given to you; seek and you will find; knock and the door will be open to you.

For everyone who asks receives; the one who seeks finds; and to the one who knocks, the door will be opened".

This passage is part of the Sermon on the mount of Beatitudes in Galilee, where Jesus teaches us about trust in prayer, perseverance, and faith. Do not get tired of pleading, of asking- for in time, the door will open.

A parable I carry in my heart and that has helped me in my faith is Luke 18:1-8 (NIV): Jesus told his disciples a parable to show them that they should always pray and not give up.

"In a certain town there was a judge who neither feared God nor cared what people thought," he said. "And there was a widow in that town who kept coming to him with the plea, 'Grant me justice against my adversary".

For some time he refused. But finally, he said to himself, 'Even though I don't fear God or care what people think, yet because this widow keeps bothering me, I will see that she gets justice, so that she won't eventually come and attack me!'".

And the Lord said: "Listen to what the unjust judge says.

And will not God bring about justice for his chosen ones, who cry out to him day and night? Will he keep putting them off?

I tell you; he will see that they get justice, and quickly. However, when the Son of Man comes, will he find faith on the earth?".

It is a profound teaching about constant faith and trust in God's justice, even when it seems not to come, and even more when the world seems unjust.

My migrant brothers and sisters: do not lose faith, do not stop believing, do not lose hope and do not stop trusting in the power of love.

On the other hand, to neighbors, to brothers in faith who encounter migrants on their path, I ask for patience and love. Share the love of Jesus Christ, as described in:

1 Corinthians 13:1-8a (NIV):
1. If I speak in the tongues of men or of angels, but do not have love, I am only a resounding gong or a clanging cymbal.
2. If I have the gift of prophecy and can fathom all mysteries and all knowledge, and if I have a faith that can move mountains, but do not have love, I am nothing.
3. If I give all I possess to the poor and give over my body to hardship that I may boast, but do not have love, I gain nothing.
4. Love is patient, love is kind.
   It does not envy, it does not boast, it is not proud.
5. It does not dishonor others, it is not self-seeking, it is not easily angered, it keeps no record of wrongs.
6. Love does not delight in evil but rejoices with the truth.
7. It always protects, always trusts, always hopes, always perseveres.
8. Love never fails.

What kind of Christians and believers do we want to be? What kind of humans do we want to be? That is the question we must ask ourselves, which we must reflect.

What kind of believers do we want to be? Those who attend mass or service twice a week, who create closed communities (cults) and forget the pain of their migrant brothers? Who makes religion a business with the most vulnerable, the neediest, the weak, the poor, those who miss the sense of belonging to a community?

Let us remember that, at some point, we too have been foreigners.

Therefore, I exhort the true Christian people, the believers who know and follow the true message of love of Jesus Christ, to pray, ask and plead for migrants, and to share the compassion to which they are called.

Likewise, for those who believe in themselves superior, whether by social status, education, money, or skin color, let us remember two things:

We are all equal inside and we all have an expiration date.

In the end, the only thing that remains is the work we did out of love for others. Everything material will fade. Even great kings and kingdoms have ceased to exist. Everything passes. Let us live by example, not just by what we preach, as the gospel of Matthew teaches us: "I was hungry, I was thirsty, and you helped me".

Final Reflection

History

Before the United States of America existed as a nation, in this territory, these lands were already inhabited, they were the home (and still are) of the original Indigenous peoples, known as Native Americans, with diverse cultures, languages and ways of life. They were and are the true owners of these lands. They lived here long before ships arrived from Europe and eventually it was, they who, over time, were called "savages", when in reality what was savage was what was done to them, but some history books for many years have told us a different story.

Starting in the 17th century, the English arrived, along with other Europeans like the Dutch and French, mainly seeking religious freedom, escaping from a crown that oppressed them, seeking freedom, economic opportunities or escaping persecution. They founded colonies, like the famous 13 British colonies, which would eventually form the core of the country.

In the 19th and 20th centuries, other great migratory waves arrived:

The Irish, especially during the great potato famine of the 1840s, fleeing poverty and driven by hunger. The Germans and Scandinavians, in search of land and better living conditions.

The Chinese and other Asians, primarily during the gold rush (starting in 1849) and for the construction of the transcontinental railroad. Unfortunately, they faced discriminatory laws like the Chinese Exclusion Act of 1882.

The Italians seeking opportunities, the Jews fleeing persecution, it was between the late 19th and early 20th centuries that they arrived in cities like New York seeking work, refuge, and a dignified life.

In the 20th century, with changes in immigration laws (especially after 1965), migration from Latin America grew —especially Mexico, Central America, and the Caribbean— as well as from countries in Asia and Africa, which transformed the United States into a truly diverse nation.

All seeking the same thing: a place to begin, a better life, a place to work, to dream, to live in peace.

Perhaps the narrative is different because they want to forget, change or erase the history of the United States, but the truth is that this is a country of migrants, this nation was built by migrant hands, by men and women who perhaps didn't speak English, but understood the language of the common good and work.

This country was raised with the tired feet of those who crossed borders, seas, and deserts... with the dream of finding here a new beginning and that is exactly what makes this nation great and powerful.

We, the migrants, are not a threat.
We do not come to destroy, nor to steal,
nor to cause chaos.
We come to build, to plant, to give.

Evil has no nationality, no passport.
Violence, cruelty, selfishness... are human evils.

And they cannot be attributed only to the one who comes from outside, to the migrant.

I remember that, during one of the recent migration crises, while helping at a shelter in a sanctuary city, I met a young mother who had just given birth. She mentioned that she felt weak, dizzy, that she did not feel well, so we decided to call 911 as it was protocol.

The paramedic who arrived was a white man, he never looked at her, never spoke to her, never touched her. He only said with coldness and anger: "Follow me".

While observing that scene —the coldness with which a paramedic treated a young migrant who had just given birth and felt ill— I understood even more why it was necessary to draft this book.

Not from a technical or legal point of view. Not with figures or statistics. But from inside the heart outward. Because sometimes eyes are quick to judge what they see, but the heart does not always understand what has not been lived.

This book is born from love, from pain, from hope. But it is also born as a bridge.

A bridge between those of us who have migrated and those who do not fully understand what it means to leave your country, your language, your family, your roots... out of necessity.

A bridge to explain that being a migrant is not an act of rebellion, but often an act of survival. That no one leaves everything they love for pleasure, but for love. For love of their children, their parents, life itself.

I also want to thank all those companions, friends, people from other cultures and nationalities, especially Americans, who have extended their hand to us, who have shown understanding, empathy, and respect. Their kindness feeds our faith and reminds us that love and humanity have no borders.

Sometimes they ask me why migrants do not arrive "legally." Why don't they get in line? Why do not they wait for "their turn."

The answer is:

Because there is not always a line.

Because the legal door is often closed.

Because immigration treaties change over the years and leave millions out.

Because if your child were hungry today, you would not wait for an appointment five years from now.

In writing this book, I do not seek your pity. Pity reduces people to their suffering; empathy, on the other hand, recognizes their dignity and humanity. What I ask for is empathy and understanding —two very different things. I ask that you listen to our voices, so often ignored or distorted by political speeches, incomplete news, or inherited stigmas.

If there is one message I want you to carry with you from these pages, it is this: When you come home and step into your clean bathroom, with privacy and without hurry... when you sit down to a warm dinner, when you embrace your children, and when you finally lie down in your soft bed, with fresh sheets and comfort —pause for a moment.

Remember that countless migrants do not share that same certainty, yet their dignity, their hopes, and their humanity are no less than yours.I hope you never have to live it, because leaving your country, your family, your home... is something deeply painful and often only another migrant can understand the weight that carries.

If we are able to speak about migration through the lens of humanity, then yes —we will be planting the seeds of change. Changes that not only benefit migrants, but society as a whole.

We migrants never forget our roots,
Nor do we lose sight of where we long to go.
But in between, we fight- every day-to belong.

We, the Migrants.

Epilogue

Love for Mexico (or your country of origin) from a distance is something constantly experienced by those of us living abroad.

Every time I share a video of my father's beloved hometown, I am reminder of his dream to return and rest there. But like so many migrant souls, he fell asleep far from his Mexico.

I see it in myself and in so many migrants, every time we travel to our country seeking how to help, what to bring, or how to advocate for change, often with our own resources.

Likewise, upon returning, we are overwhelmed by an emotional hangover: that mixture of joy for coming back and pain for not being able to stay and do more.

I have carried Mexico in my heart all these years. We migrants always carry it, even when we are sometimes not understood or not received with the same love.

Sometimes our own compatriots believe that, because we live in the north, drive big trucks and send dollars, we are doing well. But it is not always like that.

In 2024 I participated in a few binational assemblies with the objective of raising awareness about what life is really like for Mexicans abroad. In one of those assemblies, in Hidalgo, a woman took the microphone after having listened to the reality of migrant life and shared the following:

"Probably the school my children attend, the books they study will exist thanks to you, migrant brothers and sisters".

That has been one of the most moving and perhaps truest comments I have heard. Let us remember that remittances in 2024 even surpassed the automotive industry and tourism. That money is not just numbers: it sacrifices, it is absences and love for a land we never forget.

From here I call to the Mexican government —and also to the governments of our sister countries: such as Colombia, Venezuela, Nicaragua, El Salvador, Honduras, Guatemala, Argentina, and others— not to limit their recognition of us to be called "Heroes" in beautiful speeches and commemorative days.

What we need is not just praise, but real opportunities: access to dignified employment, pathways for professional growth, and the chance to secure decent housing for our families. Facilitate our procedures when we arrive in our country upon return.

Recognize that many of us have been working for 30 or 40 years without documents or benefits, that in our old age, we will not be turned away.

In 1986, under the Ronald Reagan administration, there was the last great immigration amnesty in the U.S. almost four decades have passed.

There is an entire generation of migrants who today are over 60 or 70 years old and cannot stop working, because they do not exist in the system, they are not: Neither from here, nor from there.

I remember how, at the end of 2024, a small hope arose that Mexico would possibly grant food assistance to Mexican migrants who qualified by age, to their heroes.

But the response was the usual:

"There's no money". "It's not possible". Followed by a great silence.

This is not a complaint, it is just a call for empathy and solidarity with migrants.

Open Letter to Mexico

Dear Mexico:

From afar, we continue to love you. We do it in silence —with nostalgia, with pride. We love you even when it feels like you have forgotten us.

Sometimes I ask myself: How it is possible to love a country so deeply from so far away?

The answer lies in the roots. In your living culture, in your colors, your flavors, your smells. In the nobility of your people. In the memories that are not forgotten.

Because you, Mexico, are the land that saw me born. You are my parents, my grandparents, my uncles, my brothers.

That is why, today we ask something simple but profound of you: When a migrant returns, they receive them with affection.

Do not judge them by how they dress, by the gift they bring, by whether they speak differently.

Receive them for what they are: your child who returns home. The remittances may speak for us, but they do not tell us everything. They do not speak of silence, of grief, of absence, of sacrifices. Even so, when we see the flag, hear your music, when we remember the blue of your sky, the smell of your earth,

The taste of your fruit and crave a tortilla, our hearts tighten. Because, Mexico, we are still yours.

And even when it feels like you have forgotten us, we remain here -building, planting, dreaming... of returning to you.

That is the depth of the love we have for you, Mexico. Because, although we left, we never completely left.

And we only hope that, someday, you will return to us. With affection. With justice. With dignity.

We, the migrants.

Migrant Glossary

Birth Certificate (Mexico)
Official document that registers a person's birth in Mexico. For returning migrants, it is sometimes the first step in reconstructing their legal identity.

Immigration Amnesty
Legal measure that allows undocumented people to regularize their immigration status without being penalized for their unauthorized entry or stay. In the U.S., the last major amnesty was in 1986.

Coyote / Pollero
Person who, in exchange for money, helps migrants cross the border in an unauthorized manner. While some do it out of necessity, many operate within human trafficking networks.

Immigration Detention
Arrest and confinement of people for not having valid immigration documents. It can last from hours to years. Detention conditions are often inhumane.

Documents / Papers
Terms used colloquially to refer to legal residence, visa, or citizenship in the United States. Having "papers" means having regular immigration status.

Modern Slavery
Extreme working conditions where the worker is exploited, underpaid, and has no rights, often under threat of deportation. It especially affects undocumented migrant workers.

Green Card
Colloquial name for the permanent residence card in the United States. It does not grant citizenship but allows legal living and working.

Citizen Children
Children born in the U.S., with automatic citizenship by birth, even though their parents are undocumented.

INE (Mexico)
Official Mexican identification (formerly IFE). It is essential for voting and conducting procedures in Mexico. For returning migrants, it is often difficult to recover after many years outside the country.

Undocumented
Person living in a country without legal authorization. Although frequently used, it is an imprecise and often stigmatizing term.

Immigration Limbo
State of permanent uncertainty in which many migrant people live can neither regularize their situation nor return without losing everything.

Mica
Colloquial term referring to the residence card (Green Card) or any identification document. It is also used to talk about false documents bought out of necessity.

Remittances
Money that migrant people send to their families in their countries of origin. They are a key source of income for millions of households.

Return Migration
Return of migrant people to their country of origin, whether by their own decision, deportation, old age, or lack of opportunities in the receiving country.

Social Security Number
Number necessary to work legally in the U.S. Without it, it is almost impossible to access formal employment, education, or credit.

Without Papers
Common expression among migrants to describe the lack of legal immigration status.

Visa

Document that allows temporary entry to a country. Obtaining a work, study, or tourist visa is exceedingly difficult for many people in Latin America.

Paper Doors. A Humanitarian Lens on Inmigration

This book was printed in August 2025,
in a limited edition of 300 copies.
Printed by Trauco Editorial
Prolongación Colón 155. Int. 115
(52) 33.32.71.33.33
Tlaquepaque, Jalisco

TRAUCO
Editorial